A Sailor's Life
In World War II

Z. W. "Ski" Kowalewski

Z. W. "Ski" Kowalewski E-8 NAP USN RET

TORPEDO SQUADRON VT-8

ISBN 978-1-888215-67-0
Library of Congress Control Number: 2016958414

Fathom Publishing Company
P.O. Box 200448
Anchorage, Alaska 99520-0448
Telephone 907-272-3305

www.fathompublishing.com/#asailorslife

Printed in the United States of America

Thank you

Thank you to Connie Taylor, Fathom Publishing Company,
and to my very able proofreader.

Contents

Foreword

This is the story of a true American hero, one of a small group of Americans from every part of the country who joined Torpedo Squadron Eight in the early days of the Second World War. Through a combination of courage, sacrifice, and fate, these men helped to change the course of history at the momentous battles of Midway and Guadalcanal. Their story is truly one for the ages.

As you will find in this book, Ski's story did not stop there. He has had a wonderful and fulfilling life both in war and peace. It was a privilege to write about him and the men he served with in my own book, *A Dawn Like Thunder: The True Story of Torpedo Squadron Eight*.

As Americans we are all indebted to him and his squadron mates for helping to defeat an enemy against all the odds that was intent on enslaving the rest of the world. Thank you, Ski.

Enjoy this great read.

Bob Mrazek

October 2016

Introduction

At the start of World War II, many young men answered the call to serve their country by enlisting in the military. This is the story of the Naval career of one of those men.

Ski Kowalewski and his father, Joseph Kowalewski.

PBM Martin Flying Boat in Norfolk, Virginia.

Leonard Blank and Shanghai Ed

October 1941

One of the campaign ribbons issued for service in the Pacific area during World War II was golden in color. It stood for the golden opportunity offered to the youth of America to serve in the armed forces of the United States.

I took advantage of this opportunity and enlisted in the U.S. Navy. The prospect of carrying a rifle in some muddy foxhole, if drafted, did not enter into my decision.

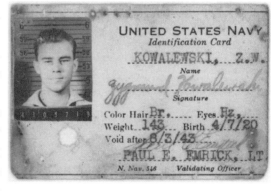

They must have needed shipboard radio operators badly. I, with no special talents, was selected to attend one of their schools. We were trained to copy Morse code, message traffic, routing, etc. The school was six weeks long and after completion, we were able to copy at 18 WPM. Eighteen words per minute was the speed used by the Navy to send Fox Schedules. Fox Schedules was the method used by the Navy during WW II to control all ship movements.

The Navy had two powerful broadcast stations. One was located in Washington, D.C., and the other in California. All Navy ships copied Fox on a twenty-four hour basis. If you missed a Fox schedule, you could get it from any other ship in the fleet. All Fox was sent coded other than a message like, "Sailor Jones, you are the proud father of a boy." Very highly classified messages were delivered by personal carrier. An example of this would be atomic bomb information.

About a week before graduation, a Navy Lieutenant recruited the class asking for volunteer aircraft gunners. Forgetting the warning not to volunteer for anything, I raised my hand. Leonard Blank also raised his. The fact that we would be getting 20% more pay did not enter into my decision.

I reported to VP-74, a twin-engined PBM flying boat squadron. I was assigned to plane #7 as second radioman in training.

Ski on guard duty VP-74, Norfolk, Virginia.

If you wanted to go on leave, you submitted a "chit." If approved by the executive officer, you were on your way. I got approval and air hitchhiked my way to Rockford, Illinois, on ten days leave.

After ten days, I reported back. I looked for plane #7 but it was nowhere to be found. "Where is plane #7?" "Oh, it flew into a mountain in Argentia, Newfoundland, all on board were killed." I dodged that bullet. I was assigned to the radio gang and another aircraft.

One day the radio gang chief received a request for a volunteer for Torpedo Squadron 8. It was referred to as a suicide squadron. No one wanted to volunteer. "Who are you going to send Chief?" "I'm sending Leonard. He is always late, screwing up, giving excuses. I can never rely on him. I'm sending Leonard."

Leonard was something else: very smart, platoon leader in radio school, always got the best deals on top of everything. He was referred to in the Navy as a "sea lawyer." Leonard looked like Tyrone Power, the movie star. He had girlfriends to spare. When he went to the girlie places, Leonard never had to pay.

Two days later, on the public address system I heard "Kowalewski report to personnel." I was handed a set of orders to Torpedo Squadron 8, East Field, Norfolk, Virginia. "Hey Chief, I thought you were going to send Leonard."

"Oh, Leonard can't go. His mother is sick in the hospital. He has to be there for her." I was Shanghai Ed like the early sailors in San Francisco; after a heavy drinking night, they would wake up on board a ship to China.

The story has a happy ending, however. Leonard was caught in the Admiral's wrecked car with the Admiral's wife. He was sentenced to two years in Portsmouth prison. It could not have happened to a nicer guy.

I reported to Torpedo Squadron 8 and was assigned to the radio gang. The chief in charge said, "You are the new guy, you make the coffee." I answered, "Chief, I don't drink coffee." "OK, your job will then be taking care of all the batteries in these 14 torpedo bombers." After two weeks with acid-eaten-up dungarees and minor acid burns, I was more than happy to say, "Chief, I'll make the coffee."

You may wonder about Leonard Blank. Leonard was so smart that I am sure he is now a power on Wall Street or a bank president somewhere. He may have not liked what I had to say about him.

My career in the Navy went on from there with bigger and better things for the next 20 years.

New York New York

December 1941

I started my tour in Torpedo Squadron 8. It was three months before the Pearl Harbor attack. There was an attitude of urgency about all of our training. I felt that it was known that war was coming. The Navy had recalled many reserves. I would guess that over 90% of recalls were reserves, not regular Navy. A large number of the pilots were recalled from major airlines. They were very good pilots. We radio gunners would always try to fly with them. They were the best.

There was a shortage of aircraft to train in. Our pilots were flying older, bi-wing, almost ancient planes. I recall many that were in need of fabric repair or had flat tires, etc. The aircraft bone yards were raided to give the pilots something to train with. Some were the Navy SBN, a not too successful model. When flying in the SBN dive bombers, we gunners would ride in the rear seat. Our job was to call out altitudes during the dive.

Pilots were known to be locked on the target and would fly into the ground. We would call out altitude changes: 15 thousand, 10 thousand, nine, eight, seven, six, FIVE THOUSAND, FIVE THOUSAND, FIVE THOUSAND.

USS Hornet CV-8, Norfolk, Virginia.

PULL UP, PULL UP. You could feel the rapid air pressure changes in your ears. It was exciting, to say the least.

The main part of the squadron trained with the older, but war-ready, Douglas TBD. They were ready to go when called. I, with the late comers, was not in the main group.

On one day off, I visited the Portsmouth Navy Yard. There, tied to a dock, was a British aircraft carrier: His Majesty's Ship _____. One side of it was completely blown out. "Hey, there are dead guys in there. These Germans are playing for keeps." This brought the war thing closer to our minds. Remember, this was before the USA entered the war. We were repairing British warships in the USA.

December 7, 1941. A day of infamy President Roosevelt called it. I was on liberty in Norfolk, Virginia. The call went out for all military to report to their units. We set 30-caliber machine guns on the roof of the hangar and stationed a 24-hour guard on the hangar entrance.

Frantic actions were started to load the USS *Hornet* CV-8 with food, bombs, supplies, and some airplanes. The flyable planes would land aboard after the carrier got underway. The loading went on 24 hours per day. We had short breaks to sleep, with meals at the site. There was some talk of someone over-leave. They said that he got punished like "wine and cake," meaning bread and water for meals and a full meal every three days. "Boy, I don't want that to happen to me." In two days, the *Hornet* CV-8 departed for the Pacific via the Panama Canal.

The Navy was getting the new Grumman TBF-1 torpedo bomber from the Grumman Aircraft factory located in Beth Page, Long Island. I was fortunate to be selected to remain in Norfolk and be part of the pickup team. With the main squadron gone, we were designated as Torpedo Squadron 8, Detachment Alpha.

USS Hornet CV-8 underway, Pacific Ocean.

Unfortunately, the original squadron attack force was all shot down in the Battle of Midway by Zero fighters. There was one survivor, Ens Gay. He witnessed the battle from a rubber raft. I was lucky to be selected to remain in Norfolk. I dodged the bullet the second time.

Life at Grumman was a dream. We were put up in the Garden City Hotel. This is where Mrs. Roosevelt stayed when she toured Long Island. We were guests of Grumman Aircraft. When you went to breakfast, you just signed; the bill was paid by Grumman. If you wanted to go to New York, you just called the factory driver. I went to New York.

Ski with shipmates Buddy Velasquez and Bibb.

The driver suggested a lesser-type hotel. In the elevator, the operator asked, "Would you like some female companionship?" I don't remember my answer. We could get low cost tickets at the USO. I got tickets to a Glen Miller concert. There was Glen Miller, Tex Beneke and his sax, and all. It was quite a treat.

We spent the days touring the factory and getting familiar with the new airplane. We started to ferry the new planes to Norfolk. After training, we were to deliver them to Pearl Harbor to the original squadron.

When checkouts were finished, we started to fly to California by way of Birmingham, Alabama. Birmingham was Lieutenant Commander Larsen's hometown so we made an overnight stay there. The whole town turned out to see the big powerful new torpedo bombers. We slept in the airplanes and used the terminal toilet facilities. Some of the boys entertained some local girls in the airplanes.

We finally arrived in Alameda, California, by way of Birmingham and San Diego. We shipped the planes via transports and the crews went on whatever was available. I went on the Pyro. The Pyro was an ammunition ship. We were loaded with hundreds of bombs, thousands of rounds of ammunition. The standard joke was, "they issued you a parachute instead of a life jacket."

We arrived in Pearl Harbor with the new aircraft. We missed the delivery. The original squadron had left the day before for the coming battle of Midway.

Our squadron was ordered aboard the USS *Saratoga* CV-3, not the USS *Hornet* CV-8, our original aircraft carrier.

I Dodged the Bullet

Our new torpedo bombers were transported to Pearl Harbor and the crews arrived there by various means of travel. I boarded the Pyro, an ammunition ship.

The squadron was designated Torpedo Squadron Eight (VT-8), now "Detachment Alpha," and was readied on the Pearl Harbor Naval Base on Ford Island. We were surrounded by the remains of some of the ships damaged by the Japanese air attack. The exposed hull of one of the ships was close by in the waters of the harbor.

Torpedo Squadron 8, Detachment Alpha, commanded by Lt. Commander Harold "Swede" Larsen, was ordered to send six of the new torpedo bombers to Midway Island. We all asked, "Where is Midway?" Some island in the Pacific. We all volunteered. It would be good duty. Lay on the beach, get a sun tan, fly searches and get out of this damned war. Fortunately, I was not selected. All but one of the six aircraft that were sent were shot down by Zero fighters during the Battle of Midway.

There was one aircraft that came back badly shot up. The hydraulic system was damaged and the compass was not working, along with other damage. The plane landed with damaged landing gear and gunner Sea1c Jay D. Manning dead in the 50-caliber turret. The pilot, Lieutenant Albert K. "Bert" Earnest, and tunnel gunner RM3c Harry H. Ferrier were wounded. Bert was awarded the Navy Cross by Admiral Nimitz.

I dodged the bullet for the third time, not going with those six planes.

The USS *Hornet* CV-8 was ordered to proceed to the Battle of Midway area. There was not enough time to qualify the pilots in the new Grumman TBF-1 torpedo bombers.

TBF - 1 No: 00387 CRASH 'SUVA" FIJI ISL. 7/30/42 KOWALEWSKI IN WATER TOP CENTER

Evart's Avenger about to sink on July 30, 1942, Ski Kowaleswki shows his swimming ability after the crash. Signatures are those of well-wishers at an Eagle River, Alaska, Veterans event in 2015 hosted by Mr. and Mrs. Bill Cook, an Eagle River attorney.

Crash of TBF-1 BUNO:00387

July 1942

On board the USS *Saratoga* CV-3 northwest of Guadalcanal Island, we had been at sea for about fifty days. The ship was sending an aircraft to Tonga Tabou, Fiji Islands. It was to pick up mail and other tasks. I was going as part of the crew. We were paid regularly while at sea and we were all loaded with cash. Tonga offered a place to spend some of it. Most of the crew gave me money to buy things. I asked, "What should I buy?" "Anything." I had collected over $2,000. It was in a big roll in my dungaree pocket. I had a very large crowd of sailors watching their $2,000 making a safe departure.

A Navy aircraft has a tailhook at its tail end. It is lowered and raised by an electric motor in the pilot's cockpit. It has up, neutral, and down positions. We started our takeoff roll. The tailhook bounded over most of the bow arresting cables, but snagged the last cable. This reduced the takeoff speed so we stalled straight into the sea.

We were armed with four 500-pound depth charges. My first thought was that "if these depth charges tear loose and go to their pressure depth, they will explode." I wanted to get away from the aircraft but fast. When we first hit the water, I was thrown forward and got struck with something under the left eye. I saw some stars but was not knocked out. I bolted out of the seat with the seatbelt still attached. It slammed me back into it. I released the seatbelt, leaped out on the right wing, ran the length, and dove into the sea. I sank to about 12 or 15 feet down. I remember looking up at the surface of the crystal clear Pacific Ocean. I felt the salt water irritating the cut under my left eye.

Pulling my toggles on my "Mae West life jacket," I bobbed to the surface. Observers on the carrier said that I won the 100 yard free style getting away from that plane. The depth charges did not tear loose and did not explode. The pilot had left the electric tailhook switch in neutral and the tailhook worked its way out on takeoff. The other two crew launched the emergency raft from the aircraft.

I remember the ship passing by me. It looked like a ten-story iron building. I expected a suction from the propellers, but there was none.

9

I swam to the rubber raft. The raft was picked up by the following destroyer. It is called the "plane guard." It is always on duty during flight operations. To get aboard the destroyer, you had to climb a rope net or ladder. A sailor yelled to me. I expected something like, "Are you okay? Can I help you?" Instead I got, "Hey sailor, do you want to sell your forty-five?" I felt like using it on him. You could declare the loss of your shoulder pistol as lost at sea.

We stayed on board the destroyer for four days. We were taken back aboard the carrier via the "breeches buoy." The "breeches buoy" is a canvas-type chair and is roped between ships. It is used to transfer mail, ice cream, and men between larger ships and smaller.

The next morning Lieutenant Commander Larsen, commanding officer of Torpedo Squadron 8, called to see me. I reported. "Are you alright?" I was not badly injured. I was on the flight schedule the next day.

The money was wet, but after drying out was returned to its owners. Things went back to the daily routine.

Ski was turret gunner in this model Grumman TBF-1 aircraft.

Invasion of Guadalcanal Island

August 1942

August 7, 1942, was a clear, scattered cloud day. The USS *Saratoga* CV-3 was cruising southwest of Guadalcanal Island preparing to launch aircraft to attack and support the 1st Marine Division landing on the island.

I was an aircraft gunner with a 50-caliber machine gun in one of the attacking TBF-1 torpedo bombers supporting the landing.

The flight to the island was uneventful. Upon arriving over Guadalcanal we observed a great battle over Tulagi Island 25 miles to the east. The marines were exchanging rapid fire with the Japanese land forces. Tracers and bullets were flying between both forces. The battle in the air was very hot. The American and Japanese airplanes were engaging each other. At times we would see a flaming aircraft crash into the sea.

At Guadalcanal Island, the marines were in the process of a beach landing. There was no resistance to the landing. Japanese forces on the island consisted of 600 military and a large number of civilian workers. The Japanese were in the early stages of constructing an aircraft runway. The military forces did not contest the landing. The military and civilian forces fled into the hills.

My TBF-1 torpedo bomber was loaded with twelve 100-pound bombs. We were having difficulty finding suitable targets. The pilot kept searching for targets. I was ready to just find one large target and drop all twelve bombs and get the hell out of there. Thank the Lord the Japanese Zero fighters were engaged over Tulagi and did not come after us. We were no match with our one 50-caliber gun and their six wing guns. We finally dropped the twelve 100-pounders and flew back to the ship. Four flights were made; two on the 7th of August and two on the 8th.

The Japanese made a great effort to retake the island but did not succeed. The Guadalcanal landing was the first victory on the drive to the final surrender of Japan. It was the turning point of the Pacific War that ended with the surrender of Japan on board the USS *Missouri* in Tokyo Bay.

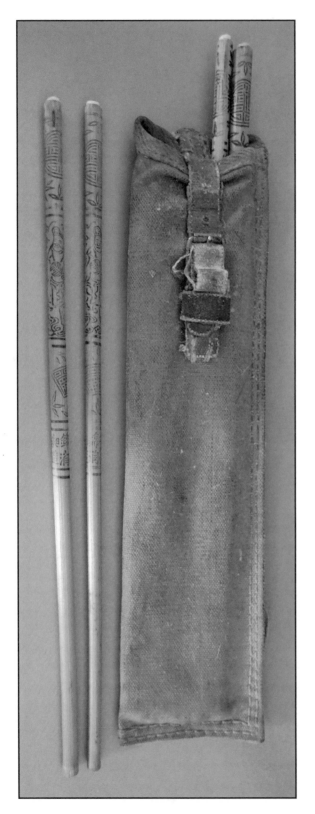

Japanese Army chopsticks and case. Note the ivory tips at the top of the chopsticks. These were issued to the Japanese Army.

Attack on Japanese Aircraft Carrier IJN *Ryujo*

August 1942

On August 24, 1942, three hundred miles northwest of Guadalcanal Island, on board the USS *Saratoga*, it was a clear, calm day, a dangerous type of weather for warships. With clear weather it is more likely that one could be discovered and attacked.

The search planes from the USS *Saratoga* had located an enemy aircraft carrier, the Imperial Japanese Navy (IJN) *Ryujo* (Dragon Horse), west of our position. All aircraft of the USS *Saratoga* were launched to attack the enemy carrier.

Fortunately for our attacking forces, the IJN *Ryujo* had launched its entire aircraft for an attack on Guadalcanal Island. This was a great advantage for the attacking force. This left the Japanese carrier in a very vulnerable position. I was a rear turret gunner on one of the attacking Grumman TBF-1 torpedo bombers. The view of the turret gunner is limited to the rear only. Very little can be seen forward. After the torpedo drop, we made a very skidding left

Japanese Aircraft Carrier "Ryujo," flagship of the strike force in the North Pacific, was sunk by US Navy forces on August 24, 1942, by aircraft from "USS Saratoga." The "Ryujo's" 16 fighter and torpedo bombers bombed Dutch Harbor on June 3 and 4, 1942.

AUG 1942

Date	Type of Machine	Number of Machine	Duration of Flight	Character of Flight	Pilot
7	TBF-1	00381	4.1	G	EVARTS
7	"	"	3.3	G	KATZ
8	"	00404	4.5	G	EVARTZ
8	"	"	4.3	J	EVARTZ
13	"	"	4.2	J	"
16	"	004 04	4.0	J	"
22	"	"	4.0	J	"
24	"	"	4.3	H	KATZ
28	"	"	2.0	J	BARNUM
30	"	00423	4.1	J	EVARTS
31	"	—	3.2	J	"
			42.0		
June 2, 1982					
Hiroechu Samejima					
Admiral, JMSDF (Ret.)					
Total time to date,				

4—0441

Ski Kowalewski's flight log book. Note the two Japanese signatures in the lower left corner. Admiral Russel was the commanding officer of a squadron of PBYs aircraft during the Aleutian Island war. I met him when he held a seminar in Anchorage, Alaska. The signatures

PASSENGERS		REMARKS	
SELF			
MAWKINS	BOMBING (HENDERSON)		
"	"	"	"
SELF - MAWKINS - LEE -	✓ " (~~AUNNUWI~~)		
SELF - MAWKINS STRUBLE	" (" "		
HAMMOND " MAWKINS	INNER AIR PATROL		
STRUBLE 1. DUNNING	" " "		
HAWKINS 11 BRADLEY	" " " "		
" FRANCIS	ATTACK JAPS — "CARRIER"		
BARTLETT 11 W.M.HALL	INNER AIR PATROL		
HAWKINS 11 POOLE	SEARCH — Subs		
SELF (SARA)	TO Espiritu Santa		

WITNESSED THREE 1,000 LB. BOMB HITS + THREE TOR-PEDO HITS — LEFT SMOKING + BURNING FIERCELY. BELIEVED TO BE—"RYUJO"

BT. FWD. — 2M1.8
THIS MO — H2.0
TOTAL — 283.8

are from Japanese pilots that flew from the IJN Ryujo when it attacked Dutch Harbor, Alaska. I asked if they were aboard the Ryujo when it was attacked and sunk. They had both been transferred and were not on board.

turn and the IJN *Ryujo* came into my view. The skidding turn is made to not present more of the aircraft to enemy gunners. I fired my 50-caliber machine gun at the guns firing at us. Tracers were filling the sky.

Fortunately, they were behind our aircraft. I observed two torpedo hits and two one-thousand pound bombs striking the flight deck. The IJN *Ryujo* appeared badly damaged.

I learned later that one of the destroyers in the IJN *Ryujo*'s task force was Commander Hara Tameichi of the IJN *Amagiria*. Commander Hara observed that not all of the aircraft of the IJN *Ryujo* had been launched. Apparently he had counted all of the takeoff aircraft. He noted that six Zero fighters were still aboard and not being utilized as air cover for the carrier. Hara wanted to advise the IJN *Ryujo* but did not want to directly question the captain. Hara knew the executive officer as a roommate at the JijuJima Japanese West Point, and advised him via blinker flashing light. Immediately, three Zero fighters appeared on deck but it was too late. The bombs were already hitting the ship.

On the return flight to our carrier, the USS *Saratoga*, I noted that we were flying past the carrier. This was noted by observing and listening to the so-called Z...B.... The Z...B... was a radio signal transmitted by the carrier, an ident (indentification) letter that is heard in each thirty degree sector. An example would be an "R" in sector 360 deg to 030 deg magnetic. Each additional thirty degree sector would have a different letter. If you heard the "R" you would know you were in the 360 deg to 030 deg sector. This would tell you to fly 180 degrees from 30 degrees to the carrier. In other words, 210 deg magnetic. We could have flown on and crashed into the sea.

The IJN *Ryujo* was left listing and burning. The ship sank later that day. The Japanese destroyer IJN *Amagiria* with Commander Hara rescued many of the survivors.

The returning aircraft from the IJN *Ryujo* had to ditch and some of the crew members were rescued by other ships. Other returning aircraft were directed to nearby island airstrips.

Aircraft Carrier USS *Saratoga* CV-3 Torpedoed

September 1942

The USS *Saratoga* was cruising northwest of Guadalcanal Island on a clear, warm day in September 1942.

We had been at sea for over sixty days and were down to two meals a day. The aircraft carrier was in a war zone. Because of this, all wooden-topped tables were stacked to one side of the compartment. This was to keep the wood splinters from doing damage to personnel in the event of a bomb strike. Meals were eaten on stainless steel punched-out-type, multi-compartment plates. Meals were eaten cross-legged sitting on the steel deck. Breakfast consisted of chili, hard crackers, canned peaches, hard boiled eggs, and coffee.

After eating, I walked out on the flight deck and into a gun tub pit, a small area around a 20mm antiaircraft gun. It was located slightly aft of the starboard beam of the ship. I was about to relax and get some fresh air when we were all alerted with the general quarters alarm. "Submarine contact. Submarine contact." The location I was in would be a poor choice in the event of a torpedo hit. I immediately leaped up onto the flight deck and ran to the rear to the area called the "fantail." Just as I reached the fantail, BLAM! There was a loud explosion. An enemy torpedo had struck the ship in the starboard beam area. I was knocked from my feet and landed on my rear end. The entire ship shook. The action was similar to a dog shedding water after a swim. A large wave swept over the deck and drenched us all. When the wave receded, the deck was littered with small shiny metal parts. We deduced they were from the gyro of the torpedo. Of course, we all scooped up the shiny parts as souvenirs.

The carrier was not badly damaged. The USS *Saratoga* had a large blister-like addition on both the starboard and port sides. This large, steel, added compartment absorbed much of the impact of the torpedo. On the top of the addition there was a large manhole-type area. The cover of this three-inch thick top was peeled up like the skin of an orange. Fortunately no one was killed. A few sailors were shaken from ladders resulting in broken legs and arms.

Due to the damage, the carrier's speed was slowed down and so prevented the airplanes from taking off. To increase speed, two cruisers were used with attached long steel cables. This brought the speed up so it would allow safe takeoffs.

It was decided to fly all aircraft to Espiritu Santo Island. With our gear stowed in the bomb bay of the planes, we took off for Espiritu. We landed there on a newly-constructed airstrip. The aircraft carrier returned to Bremerton Navy Yard, Washington, for repairs.

I was the gunner in the air group commander's plane. I was handed two message envelopes and two red streamers with sand-weighted bags. This was to drop a message on the deck of the flagship anchored in the Bay of Espiritu. I wanted to read the messages in the worst way, but they were sealed and unreadable. I would suspect that they said, "*Saratoga* torpedoed lat/long proceeding to Bremerton for repairs." No radio transmission was ever sent due to enemy tracking.

Delivering the first message was a miss and it landed in the water alongside the ship. I then directed the pilot with a right, left, and we delivered the second message onto the deck of the flagship.

We all landed safely on the Espiritu coral airstrip and settled into tents alongside the runway. It was a very lush tropical island. There were lots of papayas, limes, and small oranges for the taking. We stayed there until ordered to Guadalcanal Island for further attacks.

Night Shelling of Guadalcanal Island

October 1942

Two Japanese battleships, IJN *Kongo* and IJN *Haruna*, shelled the island of Guadalcanal on the night of October 13, 1942. It was a very dark, overcast night. We were rudely awakened by loud explosions and flashes of exploding shellfire. The island was being shelled by the IJN *Kongo* and the IJN *Haruna*. They were capable of firing 18.1-inch shells. Their primary targets were the aircraft in the vicinity of Henderson Field.

There was confusion everywhere. Numerous aircraft were seen burning, with ammunition exploding. It was a wild night. Trucks were cruising among the men for pickup to be taken to the large bomb shelter on the far side of the island. I climbed into a truck. As it started on its way to the shelter, a lone sailor yelled out, "Hey, wait for me. Wait for me." We raced for the large shelter. A Marine gun on the east shore was firing back at the two battleships. With its limited range, its shells were falling well short of the battleships.

We arrived, including the lone sailor who had called out to us, at the large, well-built shelter. We were safe from the shelling except for a direct hit by one of the 18.1-inch shells. We spent the night in the relative safety of the shelter. The shelling went on for the rest of the night.

In the morning, we stepped out into a scene of utter destruction. Planes were burning. Parts of the 18.1-inch shells were found on the ground. Our tent camp area was not directly hit but received some damage. Going back to the airfield area, I observed a torpedo on a stand that had been hit by parts of one of the 18.1-inch shells. The nose had been cracked open and black powder was spilling out onto the ground. It was strange that it did not explode from such a hit.

All of our torpedo bomber aircraft were damaged or destroyed. Many other aircraft were destroyed also. Our mechanics managed to repair two of our planes. This was done by swapping wings and tail assembly parts. The aircraft with the replacement wing started an uncontrolled roll on takeoff but was saved by quick action of the pilot.

We were now a squadron without airplanes. The Japanese ground forces were reported advancing to capture the airfield. All of the aircrews were issued rifles and ammunition to aid in stopping the advancing enemy army. Most of Guadalcanal Island is jungle, and clear access to the airfield was limited. One of the clear areas was a ridge. The Japanese were stopped there on a previous battle. It earned the title of Bloody Ridge. Bloody Ridge was well defended. The main defensive firepower consisted of 50-caliber and 30-caliber machine guns. There was also a defense of seven barbed wire fences between the enemy and the Marines.

All aircrews were transported via truck to the ridge area. I spent three nights in the trenches with the Marines. Being out of my element, I copied the actions of a Marine. When he went to chow, I went to chow. When he went to the head, I went to the head. It turned out that he was a cook but still a fighting Marine. After the three nights, we were evacuated. We were put aboard a destroyer, the USS *Henderson*, to be taken back to Espiritu Santo Island and out of the battle zone.

The destroyer was delivering 115/145 octane fuel for the island's aircraft. This was done by the use of two large barges containing many steel fuel barrels. Our fighter protection was circling overhead to screen the operation. Suddenly Japanese dive bomber planes attacked the two barges and set them on fire. One of the dropped bombs struck the stern of the USS *Henderson* killing one of our crew and others. The wounded were taken to the mess hall for treatment. We all aided with care for the wounded. One of the casualties had been hit by shrapnel. I could see moonlight through the hole in his ear. He asked for a drink. I gave him a drink of my limeade (made from limes we were able to get on Guadalcanal) that we all carried in our canteens.

All of the attacking bombers were shot down by our fighter cover but both fuel barges were destroyed by fire.

The attack occurred in the late afternoon and it soon turned to darkness. Out of nowhere, there appeared a PT boat with searchlights showing. All of our crew went aboard the PT boat for transport to Tulagi Island. Tulagi was about twenty-five to thirty miles to the east of Guadalcanal Island.

Tulagi Island had been a Japanese submarine base with maintenance shops, docks, and a unit of scout planes. Not being assigned to any duties and just awaiting transportation, I was free to roam the island. I toured some of the submarine service shops and saw some of the highly rated "long tom" torpedoes. I also found some damaged floatplanes and pried loose some of the cockpit nameplates like "gear up," "mixture rich," "flaps down," all in Japanese.

We spent about five days on the island. We could see the Japanese bombers release bombs on Guadalcanal. One day after the drop, it appeared that the island had vanished in a cloud of dust and debris. After some time, the cloud would clear and the island would still be there.

We boarded a destroyer for transport to Espiritu Santo Island and out of the active war zone. From Espiritu Santo Island, it was aboard the transport ship to the "Good Old USA."

NAVY DEPARTMENT

BUREAU OF NAVAL PERSONNEL

Washington,25, D.C.

From: Chief of x Naval Personnel.
To: CO, Composit Squadron TWELVE.

Subj: KOWALEWSKI,Zygmund Walter, ARM1c, USN
         Transmittal of Presidential Unit Citation.

Ref: (a) General Order 187 dated 3 February 1943 amended by
             Alnav 137 dated 7 July 1943.
         (b) BuPers letter Pers-650-1ae, MM/410 57 19 of 20 August 1943

1. The Chief of Naval Personnel takes pleasure in forwardingwwith his
congratulations a facsimile of the Presidential Unit Citation awarded
the FIRST MARINE DIVISION, REINFORCED for the period of 7 August to
9 December 1942.

2. In accordance with reference (a), the subject named man, who was
certified by the Commanding General, First Marine Division, Reinforced
as having actively participated in the engagements for which theor-
ganization was cited, is entitled to wear an additional blue enamel
star on his ribbon bar in lieu of the second award of the Presidential
Unit Citation.

3. A copy of this letter and citation have been made a part of the
official record of KOWALEWSKI.

By direction.

                                        G. M. STODDARD,

                                        Captain, USN,
                                        Enlisted Performance
                                                Division

Enc.
     (a) Facsimile of Presidential Unit Citation.
     (b) Blue Enamel Star.

HEADQUARTERS OF THE COMMANDER
SOUTH PACIFIC FORCE
OF THE UNITED STATES PACIFIC FLEET

    In the name of the President of the United States,
the Commander South Pacific Area and South Pacific Force,
takes pleasure in presenting the AIR MEDAL to

AVIATION RADIOMAN SECOND-CLASS ZYGMUND WALTER KOWALEWSKI, 410 57 19
            UNITED STATES NAVAL RESERVE

for service as set forth in the following

    CITATION:

        "For meritorious achievement while participating in
    aerial combat against the enemy in the British Solomon
    Islands area. During the period October 1, 1942, to
    October 23, 1942, Kowalewski, took part in repeated aerial
    attacks on the enemy as turret gunner and radioman. In
    every attack Kowalewski exhibited extraordinary gallantry
    and intrepidity while under enemy fire and at all times
    fulfilled his duties with intelligence and great courage.
    By his perseverance and devotion to his duties, Kowalewski
    enchanced the success and efficiency of the numerous attack
    missions made by his unit while operating in this area
    under extremely adverse conditions."

                    W. F. HALSEY,
                Admiral, U.S. Navy.

    Temporary citation.

THE SECRETARY OF THE NAVY

WASHINGTON

4 February 1943

Cited in the Name of

The President of the United States

THE FIRST MARINE DIVISION, REINFORCED

Under command of

Major General Alexander A. Vandegrift, U.S.M.C.

CITATION:

"The officers and enlisted men of the First Marine Division, Reinforced, on August 7to9, 1942, demonstrated outstanding gallantry and determination in successfully executing forced landing allaults against a number of strongly defended Japanese positions on Tulagi, Gavutu, Tanambogo, Florida and Guadalcanal, British Solomon Islands, completely routing all the enemy forces and seizing a most valuable base and airfield within the enemy zone of operations in the South Pacifiz Ocean. From the aboved period until (9 December, 1942, this Reinforced Division not only held their impottant strategic positions despite determined and repeated Japanese Naval, air and land attacks, but by a series of offensive operations against strong enemy resistance drove the Japanese from the proximity arf of the airfield and inflicted great losses on them by land and air attacks. The courage and determination displayed in these operations were of an inspiring order."

Frank Knox
Secretary of the Navy

Japanese Zero fighter wing part, note the smooth rivets. This piece was part of the Japanese Zero fighter "red meatball."

Japanese Zero fighter wing part.

Ski's prayer book was damaged by shrapnel during a Guadalcanal Island battleship shelling. It was stored in his sea bag in his tent. The shrapnel penetrated the cover and sixty pages. There are no atheists in foxholes.

Back in the Good Old USA

March 1943

Arriving in San Diego from the Pacific war zone, the first order of business was to get all of my uniforms and issued gear replaced. We could claim any losses caused by enemy action. The uniform issue clerk asked, "What did you lose?" My answer, "I lost everything." I had my sea bag shattered by the battleship shelling. I replaced my entire standard issue gear.

There were a few days off with no duties. We would hang out in the "gedunk," Navy slang for snack shop. One day while I was enjoying a banana split, the movie star Edward G. Robinson arrived there. He was working in a movie titled "Deep Six." He was dressed in the blue Chief Petty Officer uniform. He really looked the part. He announced to all hands, "Come on boys, the treat's on me." He bought a treat for everyone in the room.

I was granted thirty days leave and flew to Rockford, Illinois. I was treated like a big hero arriving back from the Pacific war. There was a picture and large article in the local paper.

Brother Eugene and Ski at San Diego, California, reunion.

"To Zig, As in all other things, a group with fighting heart & on the ball at all times, because he works and fights for the cause and not for himself, now and always may luck stay with him. Your Bro. Hogan."

Home on leave, Zygmund Kowalewski, 21, naval avia tion radioman third class, is called upon to adjust fam ily radio. He is son of Mr. and Mrs. Joseph Kowal 1240 Seminary street. (Register-Republic photo.)

Young Rockford Flier Gets 2nd Hero Award

A young Rockford flier today had received his second decoration for gallantry in less than six months. Zygmund Walter Kowalewski, 22, aviation radioman, second class, was among eleven officers and enlisted men awarded decoration and citations by Rear Admiral Frank D. Wagner in ceremonies yesterday at the Sand Point naval air station, Seattle, Wash.

The son of Mr. and Mrs. Joseph Kowalewski, 1230 Seminary street, he was awarded the air medal for heroism in action in the Solomon islands area.

Kowalewski, who earlier was awarded the Silver Star following the battle of Midway, was aboard the aircraft carrier Hornet when Brig. Gen. Jimmy Doolittle's squadron took off from "Shangri-La" to bomb Tokio a year ago.

The Rockford aerial gunner-radioman was a member of the Hornet's aviation unit from the time it was commissioned in 1941 until the carrier was sunk in the southwest Pacific last summer. Following the Hornet's loss he transferred to another carrier, and when the latter was damaged, he was a member of the aviation unit assigned to Guadalcanal while the ship was being repaired.

Grounded when his torpedo squadron suffered plane losses, he served in the front lines with the marines. Later in the Solomons planes from his carrier were credited with sinking 14 Jap ships and his plane accounted for the destruction of an enemy cruiser.

A member of the Rockford unit of the naval communications reserve, he was called to active duty in January, 1941.

His brother, Eugene, who was called to duty in December, 1940, was a radioman aboard a destroyer until he was transferred last February to the sub-chaser school at Miami, Fla., and later assigned to sea duty. *1943*

Newspaper clippings from the Rockford, Illinois, newspaper, The Register-Republic.

Brings Home Jap Souvenirs

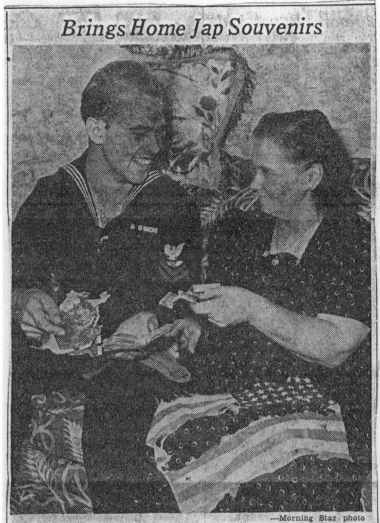

—Morning Star photo

Zygmund Kowalewski, naval aviation radioman home on leave from combat duty on an aircraft carrier in the southwest Pacific, smiles as he attempts to convince his mother, Mrs. Joseph Kowalewski, 1240 Seminary street, that the 50-yen Japanese note she is holding is worth $12.50 in American money. Across her lap is a bomb-torn flag belonging to the young sailor.

1943

Famed Torpedo Squad Member Home on Leave

A young Rockford aviation radioman is a member of torpedo squadron eight, virtually wiped out in the battle of Midway and then reorganized to exact a fearful vengeance from the Japanese in the Solomons, it was disclosed today.

He is Zygmund Walter Kowalewski, 22, son of Mr. and Mrs. Joseph Kowalewski, 1240 Seminary street, who possesses the silver star for gallantry in action in an attack on an enemy ship in the southwest Pacific and the air medal for meritorious achievement in sinking a Japanese cruiser off Gualadcanal in October, 1942. He was again recommended for the silver star early this year for heroism as a result of combat duty with the marine corps on Guadalcanal.

The squadron, whose original motto was "Attack," adopted "Attack and Vengeance" after the battle of Midway.

Kowalewski, an aviation radioman, first class, is now stationed in the United States receiving additional training. *1943*

The thirty days' leave was over. I flew to Seattle, Washington, to my next duty station. I had been given three choices: San Diego, San Francisco, or Seattle. I chose Seattle.

It was the farthest away from this blankety-blank war. I had made a good choice. I arrived at the Sand Point Naval Air Station. It was located close to the main part of Seattle. It was a great place for sailors. They were an uncommon type of servicemen there. The location of the Boeing aircraft factory was a plus also because of the many female employees.

The Navy staged USO service dances often. That is where I met my future wife, Patricia. She and her friend Betty were in nurses' training at Swedish Hospital. Pat and Betty used to sneak out after hours to attend the dances. About a year later, I married Patricia and Betty married Bill Casey.

Sand Point was a great duty station. I was ordered to the VC-34 utility squadron. The squadron was to supply aircraft and supplies, as needed, to the fleet. We were ordered to deliver six OS-2U Kingfisher sub hunter aircraft to Dutch Harbor, Alaska. I was the radio operator on one of the aircraft. Flying to wild and unknown Alaska turned out to be quite a trip. Our first overnight stop was Ketchikan, Alaska. It was a typical fishing town. Sailors were rare visitors there and we were treated royally. Free beer, drinks, king crab dinner with crackers and mayonnaise for $1.25. The next overnight was to Kodiak, Alaska. Flying into Kodiak was very difficult due to weather. Breaking out of the clouds, we were staring into a massive mountain.

Our stay in Kodiak was five days due to weather. Two days we started out and returned. We stayed in a barracks with some of the station personnel. One night we had to tie one of the guys in his bunk. He drank too much of the torpedo alcohol (torpedo juice). Torpedoes are powered by an alcohol motor. It is denatured alcohol and potent stuff. By filtering, it somehow became something they were able to drink. None of our crew participated.

Out of Kodiak, it was on to Cold Bay, Alaska. The flight took us over some wild country. Off shore at Cold Bay, we sighted a carcass of a whale being eaten by two massive grizzly bears. They scattered when we flew over. The weather was a bit cold and we had some problems starting the engines. The shotgun-type starters did not work well in cold weather.

I reported to base operations to file our arrival. There were Navy PBY-5A flying boats operating from the main runway. After two nights, we departed for Dutch Harbor. The weather was clear but the turbulence was terrible. On our approach into Dutch Harbor, I found my loose radio parts floating in mid-air. Dutch Harbor was known as the "williwaw" center of the world. A williwaw is a warm wind blowing during Alaska's winter. We delivered our six OS-2U anti-sub aircraft.

We flew a DC-3 transport back to Seattle. We made one overnight in Kodiak and then on to Seattle. The trip to Dutch Harbor took two weeks. The trip back took two days. It was great to be back in Seattle.

1943

Bombing Japs Before Breakfast Is Favorite Pastime Of Naval Fliers

Bombing the Japs "before breakfast" is the favorite pastime of navy fliers in the southwest Pacific theater of war, according to 22-year-old Zygmund Kowalewski, an aviation radioman and gunner attached to an aircraft carrier credited with sinking 14 enemy ships and engaging in 40 attacks in recent months.

Kowalewski, who arrived here yesterday to spend a short leave with his cousins, Mr. and Mrs. Joseph Kowalewski, 1240 Seminary street, brought with him a large collection of interesting souvenirs from the Guadalcanal area. Among the souvenirs is the gray cap of a Jap air corps captain named 'small mouse" who was shot down in battle.

Also in Kowalewski's collection are samples of Japanese yen notes, occupational money issued in anticipation of Jap successes in the southwest Pacific, cigarets, shells, and the name plate from a Zero. More prized by the young sailor, however, are a shell-torn American flag, riddled prayer book, and photograph damaged when a 100-pound bomb ripped into his ship quarters while he was on duty in the air.

Carried Flag For Good Luck

"I always carried this small flag for good luck," said Kowalewski, "and I'm glad I wasn't where it was when that bomb hit."

The local sailor has been notified by the navy department that he is to receive a silver star medal for heroism displayed in an attack on an enemy ship.

Kowalewski reported he found actual warfare less dangerous than a mishap which occurred when a plane in which he was taking off on a "shopping trip" to Suva pancaked in the sea.

"As we took off," he related, "the tail hook on the plane caught in a bow cable on the carrier. Our plane stalled and we spilled in the sea." Members of the crew took to the water and swam away from the ship, he went on, and kept swimming until a destroyer accompanying the carrier picked them up.

Brother On Destroyer

A former student at Rockford high school, Kowalewski enlisted in the navy two and a half years ago. He left this country in April, proceeding to Pearl Harbor, and later to the southwest Pacific. On his way back to Rockford, he stopped in San Diego where he spent three days with his brother, Eugene, 18-years-old, a radioman on a destroyer. It was their first reunion in two years.

According to the young sailor, there is nothing the fliers in Guadalcanal like better than to set off early, drop their bombs on the Japs, and return in time to discuss their exploits over breakfast.

Local Sailor Has Part In Solomons Bombing

Oct 24 - 1942

A member of a navy plane's gun crew, Zigman W. Kowalewski of Rockford, twice participated in the bombing of a Japanese cruiser near the Solomon islands early in October, according to a delayed United Press dispatch released last night by the naval censor.

The Rockford aerial gunner was one of nine praised for their part in the bombing forays which left the Jap heavy cruiser a smoking shambles. The action occurred in the late afternoon of Oct. 3 when Kowalewski's squadron caught a Jap squadron about 150 miles from Guadalcanal near the island of New Georgia. His parents, the Joseph Kowalewskis, reside at 1240 Seminary street.

Heroic Torpedo Squad, Twice Cited For Valor, Goes Back Into Action

Torpedo Squadron Eight—whose personnel included a young Rockford radio operator—is back in service aboard an aircraft carrier after it had been virtually wiped out in the battle of Midway and then reorganized to claim vengeance against the Japanese in the Solomons, the navy announced yesterday.

The navy also revealed that the squadron has become the first command in the navy to receive two presidential unit citations for valor.

Zygmund Walter Kowalewski, 22, son of Mr. and Mrs. Joseph Kowalewski, 1240 Seminary street, was a member of Torpedo Squadron Eight when it won its second citation in the Solomons by smashing 14 Japanese ships.

Awarded Two Medals

Kowalewski, aviation radioman, first class, only recently was awarded the air medal for heroism as the result of sinking a Jap cruiser off Guadalcanal in October, 1942. Previously he was awarded the silver star for heroism in an attack on a Jap ship in the southwest Pacific and early this year was recommended for the silver star for bravery in action as a result of combat duty with the marines on Guadalcanal.

Kowalewski, when not selected for air combat in Guadalcanal, aided marine machine gunners and threw grenades at Jap siege forces in the front lines.

The navy revealed that Squadron Eight's first citation came for the Midway battling. Then, under command of the late Lt. Com. John Waldron, Pensacola, Fla., the squadron went out from its carrier with orders to "intercept and attack." Those orders were carried out, although all pilots and plane crews realized their fuel supplies would be exhausted before they could return to the carrier. The enemy was stopped. But only three of the officers and men of Torpedo Eight survived.

40 Attack Missions

Reorganized under Lt. Com. Harold H. ("Swede") Larsen, Collingswood, N. J., the squadron went into the Solomons with the battle cry "Attack." And Torpedo Eight did. Its record shows 40 attack missions carried out there, with one battleship, five heavy cruisers, four light cruisers, one destroyer, one cargo ship and two aircraft carriers hit by the squadron's torpedoes.

Its presidential citation for those actions came in a joint recognition for the entire first marine division which wrested positions in the Solomons from the Japanese. Other units of the division have not been identified.

ZYGMUND KOWALEWSKI

After American forces cleared Guadalcanal of Japs, Kowalewski's squadron possessed only three planes so crew members were returned to the United States. During the six weeks he spent in the Solomons area the Rockford sailor was hospitalized for a time with malaria fever.

Kowalewski was aboard the aircraft carrier Hornet when Brig. Gen. Jimmy Doolittle's squadron took off from Shangri-La to bomb Tokio more than a year ago.

Kowalewski was a member of the navy communications reserve when he was called to active duty in January, 1941, and sent to Indianapolis for radio training. His brother, Eugene, 23, who was transferred to a subchaser school at Miami, Fla., is now on sea duty. Kowalewski has been in this country since May, when he was awarded the air medal, taking further training.

1943

30

Through the Panama Canal

April 1944

The VC-34 squadron was ordered to depart from Naval Air Station, Sand Point, Seattle, to the east coast via the Panama Canal. We were to fly and land aboard the USS *Kasaan Bay* CVE-69.

The USS *Kasaan Bay* was a medium-sized carrier. It had been built in Vancouver, Washington, by the Kaiser shipyard. They were known and referred to as "JEEP" carriers. On the trip down the west coast, we stopped at the port of San Diego. The squadron aircraft flew off and landed at the El Centro Naval Air Station near the Salton Sea. It was one of the few lakes that were below sea level. The squadron trained while in the area. On one training mission at night, one of our TBF-1 torpedo bombers crashed into the lake. The pilot was killed. The elevation being below sea level may have been a factor causing the crash. Aircraft gauges are not designed to operate below sea level.

Our spot for liberty was the City of San Diego. It happened that my brother and three other friends from my home town of Rockford, Illinois, were there. We got together and went to the Division Club. The Club was a renovated movie theater and could hold about three thousand. There was a big dance band, lots of drinking, and a wild time.

We five Navy guys, who were due to be sent to the war in the Pacific and might not return, made a night of it. We were drinking straight shots with beer chasers. At about midnight, I had to make my way back to El Centro. The method was by riding the bus. On the way back, I had to get off the bus three times to throw up in people's yards. I would sit on the roadside curb and wait for the next bus. I had a hangover for four days. That cured me of drinking.

We flew aboard the carrier and sailed down the west coast to the entrance of the Panama Canal. The entrance on the Pacific side has multiple locks. To transit the canal, you enter the first lock and are lifted to enter the second, and so on until you are at the level of Gatun Lake. The lake is well above the levels of both the Pacific and Caribbean oceans.

One of the narrowest parts of the canal is named the "Culebra Cut." The carrier had power failure of the steering rudder there. All speed was reduced and stopped to prevent crashing into a solid rock wall. The problem was caused by water entering the steering motors while washing down the hangar deck.

From the Pacific Ocean, we transited the forty-mile canal on the surface of Gatun Lake. At the Caribbean side, the ship was lowered to sea level via the eastern locks.

From Panama, it was north to Quonset Point, Rhode Island. The route passed through the Cape Hatteras area. Cape Hatteras was known as the graveyard of ships for the many ships lost there. It is an area of very violent weather. The USS *Kasaan Bay* received its share. One day all hands were ordered out on deck to add more tie-down lines on the airplanes. Wave tops were breaking over the flight deck.

The ship was rising and falling fifty to sixty feet. I was surprised that I did not get seasick. The ship was a mess. Toilet water in the head area covered the deck. Lots of loose gear was thrown around. It was the worst weather I had ever experienced.

As we neared Quonset Point, we flew off to the air station. The USS *Kasaan Bay* went to the Port of Norfolk, Virginia. We trained in the Quonset area. On one of the flights, I had my third plane crash. The linkage to the throttle from the engine became disconnected. We had the option of trying for the runway or landing in the large, cold bay. We elected to land in the bay. The tower was in contact and had dispatched a rescue boat. We landed without much trouble. The water was so cold that we were unable to talk to each other. The cold took our breath away. A dentist was on his first airplane ride with us. A long-to-remember flight for him.

We continued to train. The squadron was assigned to a new mission. We were to board the USS *Card* CVE-11 for North Atlantic anti-submarine duty.

North Atlantic German Submarine Incident

July 5, 1944

The USS *Card*, a medium sized aircraft carrier, was on submarine patrol in the North Atlantic. Our mission was to keep German submarines down as much as possible. This tactic depleted their battery power and made the submarines less effective. This was accomplished by having an aircraft in the air both day and night. Submarines surface at night to recharge their batteries. If the submarine detected an aircraft, it knew it would be in danger if it surfaced.

Our aircraft were armed with an acoustic sound-seeking torpedo. The German submarines were ordered to surface at night to send vital information to Admiral Dönitz in Germany. All Navy ships were aware of this and would take direction finding bearings on all of the submarine transmissions. These bearings were sent to a central plotting location in Washington, and with triangulation the position of the submarine was located. This in turn was sent to ships in the area of the contact.

The location of the German submarine U-233 under the command of Kapitanleutnant Hans Wilhelm Steen was passed to the captain of the USS *Card*. In the task force with the USS *Card* were the destroyer escorts USS *Thomas* DE-102, USS *Bostwick* DE-103, USS *Breeman* DE-189, and USS *Baker* DE-190. The USS *Baker* engaged the U-233 in a depth charge attack. The submarine surfaced and a battle between the two commenced. The submarine launched a torpedo toward the USS *Baker*. The location of the DE was so close that the torpedo did not arm and just bounced off the hull of the ship. The DE then rammed the submarine and damaged it so badly that it sank. Thirty of the crew of about fifty escaped into the water and were rescued. One of the rescued was the captain. He was badly wounded. The rescued were transferred to the USS *Card*.

On board the USS *Card*, we all heard of the wounded captain being treated in the sick bay. The bay was just down the passageway from our quarters. We were able to peek through a small area where a screw was missing from the bulkhead. We were able to view the injured captain lying on a table being treated. We all crowded around saying, "let me see, let me see." He was given six blood transfusions, but died that evening.

On the following day, it was announced that the funeral of the fallen foe would be held. The entire ship's company, in dress blues, was in formation for the ceremony.

The prisoners were lifted from the brig by the forward elevator and proceeded to the service area. They sauntered up like a disorganized mob. They had lost all of their gear and were in borrowed tennis shoes. Not a very impressive group. After they arrived at the site of the body, one of the group sounded off loudly with the command of "ACHTUNG." The thirty survivors came to immediate attention. They were in perfect alignment and order. This had been planned and was very impressive.

The body of the captain was on a wooden-framed incline so as to allow the body to slide into the sea when the line securing him was released. He was covered with a German flag. After the reading of the service, to the surprise of everyone, the entire German group sang out three times with the salute, "SIEG HEIL, SIEG HEIL, SIEG HEIL." The canvas-covered body with extra heavy shell casing at its feet was committed to the sea.

The service was conducted by a Navy Chaplain, Lieutenant Bell. He was asked by one of the survivors who was able to speak English if he would send the recorded location where the body was committed to the widow of the deceased captain. He said he would.

The aircraft carrier USS *Card* delivered the German submarine prisoners to Boston. They were all transferred to various prison camps in the United States.

It was a privilege to be able to witness this ceremony: A part of the history of World War II.

If I had only had a video camera.

Polish Wedding

August 1944

During World War II, it was necessary for military members to get permission to get married. I arranged with Patricia Crich for us to get married in Rockford, Illinois.

Pat came to Rockford by train from Seattle, Washington. My mother was very much the "Polish mother." Upon meeting Patricia, she exclaimed, "You not Polish." After finding out what a wonderful person Pat was, they got along just fine.

It was a very Polish-style wedding. The women of the Polish community arranged and planned everything. A large church hall was secured. There were two bars, a band for dancing, and lots and lots of food and drink.

It was customary for the guests to dance with the bride and give money. We received about $2,000 in cash to start out on our married life. The celebrating lasted three days. Out-of-town visitors stayed in various people's homes. It gave them an opportunity to visit with old friends. A good time was enjoyed by all attending.

For our honeymoon, we went to Chicago for three days. My oldest sister, Pearl, was married to the top chef at the Chez Paris nightclub. We were told it was a noted hangout for the Mafia. Mike Janoski, the chef and part owner, invited us to dinner and drinks. I remember ordering a "Singapore Sling."

After our three-day stay in Chicago, Pat took the train back to Seattle and I flew back to my Navy duty station in Quonset Point, Rhode Island.

Things were routine for some time until I applied for Navy flight training.

Patricia and Ski Kowalewski leaving the church following their wedding in 1944, Rockford, Illinois.

35

Ski Kowalewski.

Accepted for Navy Flight Training

November 1944

Walking along the ramp one day, I noticed a seaplane landing. It was not an ordinary event so I was interested as to what it was doing visiting Quonset Point. It was an amphibious-type seaplane. After it lowered its wheels, it taxied up the seaplane ramp. I was curious as to who was flying it. Stepping out was a full-ranking Navy captain.

Upon closer inspection, it was none other than my Torpedo Squadron 8 flight commanding officer, Navy Captain H. H. Larsen, with whom I had served in the Pacific Area and on Guadalcanal Island. I saluted and he returned my salute. "What are you doing these days, Kowalewski?"

Captain Larsen was a graduate of the United States Naval Academy and was in the habit of addressing his men by their last names. "I am trying to get into flight training." "Have you applied?" "Yes, sir." "I am the head of the Bureau of Aeronautics in Washington at the Navy Department. Send me a copy of your application."

I immediately went to the records office and secured a copy of my application. I sent the copy to Captain H. H. Larsen, Chief of BUAIR, Washington, D.C.

Two weeks later, I received a set of orders to report to Navy flight training.

About a year later, at a squadron reunion in Pensacola, Florida, I talked to Captain Larsen. He was in a wheel chair but still very much himself. I thanked him for expediting my transfer to flight training. His answer, "I do not remember doing it."

12 September 1942

From: Commanding Officer, Torpedo Squadron Eight

To: Commander, Service Force, Pacific Fleet

Subject: Flight Training, Recommendation for.

     1. Commanding Officer's careful estimate of candidate's suitability for flight training.

REMARKS:

     Recommended for flight training for Aviation Cadet. Kowalewski has a temperament suitable for aviation pilot duty. He is an above-average enlisted man with respect to officer-like qualities, general conduct and attitude. Insofar as is known his personal character and honesty are unquestionable.

H.H. Larsen
Lieut. USN

Lieut. H.H. Larsen's letter recommending Ski for flight training.

Matola and Ski with Stearman N2S. Pre-flight Memphis, Tennessee.

Navy Flight Training

September 1945

The start of flight training was a complete physical exam. The Navy did not want to invest in you unless there was a good chance you would complete the program. There were tests for heart, lungs, depth perception, and you had to have 20/20 vision. People over six feet in height were not eligible because you had to be able to fit into some of those smaller fighter-type aircraft.

There was a college refresher course that took six weeks at Monmouth College in Illinois. It happened to be quite close to my hometown of Rockford, so I made it home a few times on weekends.

There was a small airport near the college where I rented a small airplane and instructor. This gave me a jump on the flying that would come later.

Monmouth College pre-flight class in Illinois.
Ski is in the middle of the second row.

Ski (left) at Navy pre-flight study session in Memphis, Tennessee.

After Monmouth College, it was preflight training at Memphis, Tennessee. There was a long wait before the flying part. First there was football, boxing, swimming, obstacle course, and track exercises. There were classes on weather, engines, and celestial navigation. We were trained to obtain a fix from the stars to find our location in 15 minutes. In the swimming part, you had to swim one mile in 15 minutes with your clothes on. If you did not know how to swim, you were shown how. One of the fun things was the removing of your wisdom teeth. I did not have any, so missed that pleasant activity. Finally, after all of the physical conditioning, we were going to fly airplanes.

The flying was in a Navy S2F Stearman bi-wing airplane. It was very rugged and fully aerobatic. My first instructor was a Marine pilot who flew the airplane more than I did. I resented that because I was the one that was supposed to learn to fly. On one flight, we had to put the airplane up on its side to clear some tall trees. He was such a hot pilot that he hit a wind sock and was transferred out.

On my first flight check, I received a down. This meant that I did not pass. I thought I was pretty good and this really got my attention. You were given one recheck, and I passed that one. I went on and finished without any more downs.

Finally, the day came for my solo. The Memphis airport was laid out like two dumbbells. There were two large circular areas. You could take off with the wind always on your takeoff heading. On a regular day when taking off, there would be yellow airplanes to the right, left, and ahead of you. It was like a beehive with airplanes all around

Ski Kowalewski in Navy Stearman N2S in Memphis, Tennessee.

you. On your solo day they put two large flags on your wings. When taxiing out with the green wing flags, for some reason, there was lots of space around your airplane.

Here goes. I sat there and thought, "If I push this throttle forward, I will have to get this airplane back on the ground." I made the takeoff and went to an outlying field and made two practice landings. I wanted to make a good landing upon returning to the main base.

This was against the rules. You were to take off and land at the base field on your first solo. That way in case of an accident, rescue was handy.

The Stearman S2F was a perfect trainer aircraft. Some of the maneuvers we did were falling leaf, slow roll, snap roll, inverted flying, and the ultimate, the inverted tailspin. On the inverted spin, the instructor put you in an inverted upside-down attitude and then he recovered. "Now you do me one, left and right." This was to teach you how to recover in the event you got into that position. You got to where the airplane became almost part of you. You would practice all of these maneuvers to prepare for the flight check. I made it a habit of returning to main base inverted. I would put the airplane upside down, fly until the oil pressure showed a drop, and then do it all over again. This was a confidence maneuver to get a good feel of the airplane.

Everyone in the Navy has a buddy. My buddy was Eddie Velasquez. All aircrew were instructed to designate a person to inventory their effects in the event that your aircraft was lost. I was Eddie's designated person. Later Eddie's aircraft did not return and I inventoried his effects to be sent to his family. Then one morning during formation with about seventy cadets, I spotted Eddie as one of the new cadets. I yelled out, "EDDIE! EDDIE!" and dashed over to embrace him. Eddie had not only survived but was credited with shooting down one of the top Japanese Zero fighter aces.

After completing the basic course, we were transferred to Pensacola, Florida. We were now flying the Navy SNJ. It was a much higher horsepower plane and also aerobatic. It was noted for having a wicked stalling reputation. We practiced formation flying, hooded instrument training, aerial gunnery, and field carrier landing approaches. Field carrier approaches were done with a flag-waving approach landing officer. You would approach the landing slowly, flaps down, gear down, and about six miles per hour above stalling speed. On one of my approaches, I hit what was known as a dust devil. This stalled my plane, and I did the right thing by pushing the nose down to regain flying speed. If I had pulled back, the plane would have stalled and crashed. The flag officer yelled, "What are you doing?"

After the field carrier practice, we flew to an aircraft carrier in the Gulf of Mexico and had to make six carrier landings. I made the six landings with no trouble. In fact, I thought they were not as difficult as the field carriers. You have the advantage of the 30 knots speed the ship is traveling.

Ski qualified to fly Navy PBY Catalina, Squadron 4, Pensacola, Florida.

Carrier landings were the last phase. After a final landing at main base, you were graduated and became a Navy pilot, eligible to wear those golden wings and able to fly any airplane in the Navy.

My next flying assignment was to Pensacola, Florida, and a checkout in the Navy PBY twin-engine seaplane. The training area was the bay to the south. With a seaplane, you always have to try to keep water under you. During the training, whenever you got into a position where you could not make a water landing, you were given an engine cut. You really remembered to keep water under you whenever possible.

World War II was coming to its end in 1944 and the need for pilots was less critical. I was ordered to Jacksonville, Florida, for operational flying. There, we flew the twin Beechcraft and the Douglas DC-3.

Many of the pilots wanted out of the Navy after the war's end. I elected to stay in and make it my career. I stayed and retired after 20 years of service.

Ski flew a Navy F6F Hellcat while in Norfolk, Virginia.

Naval Air Test Center

February 1951

My next duty station was the Naval Air Test Center at Patuxent, Maryland. It is located quite close to the Pentagon near Washington, D. C. All new Navy aircraft were tested there. The different tests were flight, ordnance, and electronics.

I was assigned to serve as a pilot in the operations department. Operations would provide aircraft support to all of the base flying.

A DC-3 transport crashed during takeoff. The two radial engines failed. The aircraft impacted in a wooded area and was badly damaged. The crew of three died in the crash. The plane had been fueled with JP-3 jet fuel. The DC-3 requires high test aviation fuel to operate properly. The airman that fueled the aircraft the night before had fueled it with JP-3 jet fuel instead of the aviation high test required. He was to stand trial at a court martial due to his mistake.

I had flown the DC-3 the night before and was called as an expert witness. Not knowing what type of questions they would ask, I made myself some notes. During the trial I was not allowed to use any notes. About all I ever testified to was that the aircraft had operated and flown satisfactorily that night. The airman was convicted of negligence and sentenced to two years in a federal prison.

An incident of interest was when I had been assigned as "safety pilot" flying with Admiral Pride, the head of BUAIR. It was not that the admiral was not a good pilot, rather that Navy regulations required any pilot over 50 years of age to have a safety pilot.

The admiral usually flew two flights per month, two hours each. You needed four hours of flight time per month to qualify for flight pay.

Flying as co-pilot put me there with not much to do. I dared to ask the admiral, "How did you make admiral? Did you invent something like the Momsen Lung that Admiral Momsen invented?"

He said, "No, I just did my job and one morning I woke up and was an admiral."

When the Navy received a new jet engine, it would be flown from sun-up to sun-down until it failed. These expert test pilots would not have much trouble to land, engine out, on the 13,000 foot long and 300 foot wide runway. We witnessed about one engine-out landing per month.

One additional special test was for JATO helicopter-assisted takeoff. On the first test, the JATO unit detached from its mounting and went up and damaged the rotor blades. The helicopter crashed and burned, killing the pilot.

Strategic Air Command

March 1951

When I was stationed at the Naval Test Center Patuxent River, Maryland, I was assigned to fly a Navy captain to a base in the Midwest. Naval officers of a very high rank could request and fly Navy aircraft for transportation connected with official business. Many would drive from Washington to Patuxent and thus acquire transportation. A Navy captain is not the same as an Army captain. His rank would be the equivalent of an Army colonel. The Navy captain was referred to as a "four striper" by the enlisted men.

When flying someone of this high rank, you indicated on your flight plan, in the remarks section, VIP Code-3. We were flying a twin Beechcraft. It is a twin-engined aircraft of about six passengers and requires two pilots. Pilot in command and co-pilot, or as commercial aviation would call a "first officer."

We did not have enough fuel to get to the destination of the Captain so that required that we land for refueling along the way. We landed at an Air Force base.

The control tower directed us to taxi and park in front of the administration building. There, in all of its lofty grandeur, stood a full set of colors with a large band of musicians.

Seeing all of this ceremony, I asked the Navy captain, "Do they always do this for you, when you land at an Air Force base?" He fixed his tie, slicked his hair, and buttoned up his uniform. The band started to play and then suddenly stopped.

Then the control tower directed us to taxi to the parking area. Climbing out of our aircraft, we noticed a very large four-engine, double-decked transport land and taxi to the administration building. It was the personal airplane of General Curtis LeMay, the head of the U.S. Strategic Air Command (commonly known as SAC). The tower had mistakenly thought that General LeMay was my VIP. We refueled and proceeded to our destination.

Grumman Navy UF-1 Albatross: Ski flew this model of aircraft in the Albatross Flight Incident.

R4D/DC3 flew in Coco Solo, Panama Canal Zone.

Panama Canal Zone

1954

My next duty station would be Coco Solo in the Panama Canal Zone. My wife Patricia and our four children, Steve (8), Bill (6), Kitty (4), and Jane (2), flew to Coco Solo Naval Air Station in the Panama Canal Zone. The Coco Solo station is rather small. The airport has only one runway. I was assigned to the operations department. We had access to a DC-3 transport, a twin-engine Beechcraft, and a Grumman Navy UF-1 amphibian Albatross to fly. We flew general utility flight supplies to the embassies at Guatemala; Bogota, Colombia; and Lima, Peru. At times we were asked to assist in emergencies and rescues.

Ski and Patricia with four children (l to r) Steve, Kitty, Jane and Bill.

I will describe some of the more interesting events that we were involved with.

Trip to Lima, Peru! On this trip the Navy allowed us to take our wives. That is not the usual case. The four children stayed in the duplex apartment with our part-time maid, Violet. Violet was a Panamanian with a very jolly personality. You could have a part-time maid for about $30.00 per month.

The trip lasted about three days. While there we visited a massive stone church. It was constructed of huge blocks of some type of rock. There were no doors, just an open entry. The altar was decorated with life-sized statues of the saints. You sat on hard wooden benches. The inside was dark and damp. People would enter and pray and leave at random. One of the thoughts I had while observing the large blocks of stone: it would be a bad place to be during an earthquake. Those large blocks would be hard to avoid.

Trip to Bogota! Bogota, Colombia, is the location of two of the largest emerald mines in the world, the Muzo and Chivor mines. One is owned by the government and the other is privately owned. Thinking that I might

Ski (left) and Joe Carpino (right) stand before Navy UF-1 Albatross aircraft in the Panama Canal Zone.

be in a position to purchase an emerald, I made some inquiries. I was told that you could identify a true stone if it contained a small flaw called a feather. To view this feather I had taken along a jeweler's loupe. I also was told that if the stone was a bit off color the price would be much lower. Arriving in Bogota I asked a person on the street, "Where can I buy an emerald?" The party said to go to the second floor of a certain building. I entered the building and proceeded to the upper floor. Finding the sales office, I entered a rather ordinary room with a man at a desk. "I would like to buy an emerald." The man went to a wall safe and came out with a steel box that was filled with numerous brown envelopes. He took out one and showed me a perfect large stone of excellent color. "This one is $22,000." He then showed me others. "This one is $24,000. This matched pair is $36,000." I gasped and said, "I think I have come to the wrong place." I then asked, "Where can I buy a more reasonably priced stone?" He said that vendors sold emeralds on the main street. I located a vendor and settled on a three-quarter karat stone mounted in an 18 karat gold setting for $80 U.S. dollars. It was a bit off color and had the tell-tale feather. We had it appraised at a later date. A jeweler said it was worth about $350. At today's rate, with inflation, it would be worth ten times more. It was my wife's favorite ring, and after Patricia's passing it was given to my daughter Jane.

Trip to Guatemala! Flying supplies to Guatemala, I flew the Navy UF-1 Albatross. The outdoor markets there sold interesting things. In Panama there was a man that had a greenhouse and grew orchids. He wanted me to purchase some for him. I located a vendor and purchased 18 different varieties for about $20. One of the people we delivered supplies to was "Huleo." One of his interests was the ownership of about six factories that made colored fabric. The cloth was handmade by women weaving on hand-operated looms. He sold shirts, skirts, and other articles made from this brightly colored cloth. Shopping in the downtown area we saw numerous women with sleeping children in store entryways. My wife asked the women, "Where are your husbands?" They answered, "No husband, just babies."

San Jose, Costa Rica! I flew the two-engine Cessna Beechcraft. The runway there was very short and the approach was made over some tall trees. It was a tight squeeze getting into there. On the takeoff weight I was limited to 600 pounds because of the short runway. The Navy commissary store would get its tomatoes there for about five cents per pound. One of our mechanics wanted some choice beef. You could buy filet mignon, the choice back of beef, for 28 cents per pound. The meat was sold in the open hot sun. In our hotel, we noticed a large number of news reporters. Their roster was displayed on the bulletin board. There was an alert notice that we would be warned of a hasty departure. There was some kind of uprising in progress. We were not alerted.

Control tower incident! Due to low traffic, the station did not require any regular control tower operators. At times we were assigned to the control tower. While on watch I received a distress call from six P-47 fighter planes. They had been strafing San Jose and were trying to land at Coco Solo. They had overflown our field and were south of the airport. They were asking for a compass heading back to Coco Solo. To do this they transmitted on their radio and the tower, with special equipment, could locate their position. Then they were given a compass heading, or a steer, to the airport. They were able to land at our airport. Observing them with my binoculars I noticed that they had no identification markings. No serial numbers, nothing. They were rushed and hidden in our hangar. I made an entry of the incident in the tower log. It was later removed by my superiors. The P-47 fighters were a secret CIA operation supporting an uprising in Costa Rica.

Patricia and I with the children left Panama on a Navy transport ship for New York City. Arriving there, we picked up our shipped car and drove to our next duty station in San Diego, California.

We really enjoyed our two years in the Panama Canal Zone.

Tough Navy Duty in Lima, Peru: Ski and Patricia dancing at the Embassy Club.

Navy UF-1 Albatross Flight Incident

1954 Coco Solo, Canal Zone

It was a Sunday morning and the Navy UF-1 Albatross had come out of maintenance. The plane required a flight test before being sent on a scheduled flight Monday morning.

I was called to perform the flight test. Since it was a Sunday, there were no qualified co-pilots available. I told the mechanic who had done the maintenance to get in the co-pilot's seat and we would do the one-half hour test flight.

We made our takeoff. When I selected the up lever on the landing gear, the lower plastic window filled with red hydraulic fluid. I immediately put the lever back down. The result was we had one landing gear up and one down. In this condition, we were unable to make a water landing or an airport landing.

What to do? First, you get on the air to get any help from ground sources. They have access to the manufacturer of the aircraft to learn the best things to do in such a situation.

I got on the radio with the operations officer. He asked, "Who is with you?" Long silence. I had an illegal co-pilot, the mechanic.

The mechanic disassembled a hydraulic line. This made it possible to pour in our onboard spare fluid. With me pouring the red hydraulic fluid into the opened end, and both the mechanic and me hand pumping the hydraulic pump, we dropped and locked the retracted gear. We now had both gear down and locked.

This put us with no braking and no flaps. This required a no flaps landing and no braking for stopping. I did have the reverse of both engines available to assist stopping the plane.

I made a faster than normal, no-flaps landing and kept the aircraft in the center of the runway. Using the engine reverse to stop the plane, we were down safely.

The tow truck came to tow us to the hangar. I said, "My responsibility ends right here!"

Ski Kowalewski and Hopalong Cassidy at Palm Springs Airport, California.
Hopalong is known for starring as a cowboy hero in a 1952-1954 TV series.

I Flew Hopalong Cassidy

December 1955

It was a warm bright day in December in San Diego, California. It was Christmas week. The Navy was having a big Christmas party for the children of Navy families.

Guess who had been selected to be the main attraction at the party?

None other than the big western movie star Hopalong Cassidy.

Guess who was going to fly him to and from Palm Springs, California?

None other than guess who: ME.

I was assigned to fly Hoppy from Palm Springs using a Douglas DC-3 cargo-type aircraft. The DC-3 is a two-engine airplane designed to carry about twenty-five to thirty passengers. The engines are rated at 1800 HP each. Quite a large aircraft.

You would think that operations would have assigned a more suitable aircraft. The airplane was a troop and cargo type aircraft. There were no regular seats. Passengers sat on canvas bench seats along each side of the plane.

I took off and proceeded to Palm Springs. Waiting at the terminal were Hopalong Cassidy, his pretty wife, his agent and the agent's wife.

After introducing ourselves, I asked Mr. Boyd, "Can I take your picture?" (His real name is William Boyd.)

"Come over here." He put his arm over my shoulder and we had our picture taken.

Hopalong Cassidy, the cowboy movie star, looked like one. He was over six feet tall, wide shoulders, and a narrow waist. His outfit was black with silver trimming wherever it could find a place to attach itself; two large holsters and pistols all trimmed in silver and a large cowboy hat with trimming. He wore knee-high leather boots, with spurs, of course. He looked like a real cowboy, but only for his rhinestone outfit.

His wife was much shorter, like five foot eight, blond hair, light featured face, wearing a pretty pink dress. Her shoes were black with medium high heels.

Hoppy's agent and the agent's wife were with him. His agent was of average height, appeared to be about middle-aged. He wore a dark suit, blue tie, and dark shoes. The agent's wife was rather ordinary looking but well dressed for the occasion.

I helped them board the aircraft via the narrow metal ladder, requiring some assistance. These dressed-to-the-nines folks had to sit on the canvas side row seats. Hoppy put his silver guns and hat on one of the canvas seats.

After making the takeoff, I invited Mr. Boyd to take a seat in the cockpit co-pilot's seat. He flew the plane all the way to North Island. A DC-3 is quite easy to fly when all trimmed level, and balanced pressures on the controls.

Hoppy left the cockpit and buckled himself in for the landing.

We were met by transportation, and the party left for the North Island children's Christmas party.

The trip back to Palm Springs was uneventful. They left in good spirits.

It was a great privilege to have had this experience. It is one of the few things that I have to add to my claims to fame:

I flew Hopalong Cassidy, the movie star!

Ski in pilot's seat in DC-3
at North Island, San Diego, California.

I Flew Supersonic

September 1960

At the North Island Naval Air Station in San Diego, California, there were three F9F-8 Cougar jet aircraft made available for the pilots on the staff of COMNAVAIRPAC to fly. They were required to fly a minimum of four hours to receive flight pay. These three jets were also available for base operations pilots. To qualify to fly the F9F-8, I had to read the operation manual, pass an ejection seat test, and complete a pressure chamber test. I had completed the three and was anxious to fly the jet airplane.

I learned some interesting features of jet airplane flying. The airspeed is read by the use of a Mach-1 instrument. The Mach-1 meter measures how far you are from exceeding the speed of sound. If it is flying faster than Mach-1, the plane is flying "supersonic." A new instrument in jets is the angle of attack meter. It measures the angle of attack of the airflow over the wing. It has a circular dial with green, yellow, and red sectors. If you keep the indicator in the green area the plane will not stall. When flying, the pilot tends to fly the angle of attack rather than airspeed. When wearing an oxygen mask, oxygen is fed to the pilot by an automatic bellows-type system. You get very little oxygen at sea level and progressively more as the plane climbs to higher altitudes. At about thirty thousand feet, there is one hundred percent oxygen. In addition, the cockpit is pressurized. The speed of sound at sea level and at the temperature of 59 degrees Fahrenheit is 761.2 miles per hour. At higher altitudes and lower temperatures, it is less.

My first flight was interesting. When I advanced the throttle, there appeared what looked like smoke. It was the air conditioning pressure fogging up, and it cleared quickly. This jet airplane accelerates very slowly and then progressively gains speed. Usually when passing over the far runway end, I would be traveling about 260 to 280 miles per hour. I used notes from a climb schedule from my knee pad, noting the recommended airspeeds for the altitude I was at. This was to get the best fuel rate burn.

I had flown the plane for about fifteen hours and was talking to one of the experienced pilots. He said the airplane would go supersonic. Now, this is a single-engine jet not designed or tested to ever fly faster than Mach-1.

I asked, "Have you ever done it?" He said, "Yes, a couple of times." "How do you do it?" I asked. "You climb to forty thousand feet, put her into straight down vertical dive, at full throttle, and she will go supersonic," he told me. Crazy me thought, "I will try it."

I took off and started my climb to forty thousand feet. It was a struggle to get up that high. Finally, I arrived at forty thousand. The air is thinner up there and the plane flies more sluggishly. I made it a point to be out over the ocean. I was going to create a sonic boom but not over a populated area. I pointed the nose straight down and applied full throttle. I was at an angle of about 80 degrees and was not going through the barrier. "I'm not going to do this again."

I put the nose straight down to 90 degrees. My speed seemed to hang up and hesitated to go through to over Mach-1. The airspeed jumped ahead for fifty to sixty knots and the Mach-1 meter read more than one. I know I have gone through the sound barrier. It is very quiet. It seemed that all of the sound is well behind me.

Now for the pull out. I made a gradual pull out so as to not go into a high speed stall. I recovered at about 18,000 feet. "Oh boy, she is still running." It is lucky that the engine did not flame out. I had planned for that. I had a clear field spotted and would land there with my gear up. I advanced the throttle. "Oh boy! She is still running." The refueling probe and windscreen frosted over. I made my pull out using instruments.

This was a very unwise thing to do. I was to retire from the Navy in one month. Now I had bragging rights. Not many propeller pilots can say they have flown faster than the speed of sound.

I would not do it again for one hundred dollars. Just kidding. Never again. AMEN.

Ski flew supersonic in this model of aircraft, F9F-8 Navy Cougar.

Convair C-340 Lightning Strike

1959

I departed from Anacostia Airport, Washington, D.C., for North Island San Diego Naval Air Station in a Convair C-340, a twin-engined pressurized transport aircraft. I was cruising at 18,000 feet on a dark, rainy, turbulent night. There were black cloud buildups and the sky was full of numerous lightning flashes. I was on an instrument flight plan and restricted to fly on the designated airway.

When I saw a large buildup and lots of lightning ahead, I requested a course change around the center of the dark buildup from air traffic control. The radar control center gave me a steer from due west to a southwest heading that was supposed to skirt the storm. About five minutes on the new heading, I was struck by a very bright, loud lightning strike on the nose of the aircraft. I called radar control and said, "Thanks a lot, I just got hit by lightning."

When flying under conditions like we were, you normally set the airplane on autopilot, bring the cockpit lights up to full bright, reduce speed, and try to fly through the lighter areas of the storm.

Usually before getting a lightning strike, you see what is called "Saint Elmo's fire" which is a spider-like sizzling on both side windows and at the base of the windshield. You also get a strange smell from the static electricity affecting the oxygen in the air. This produces ozone which has a distinctive odor. We received all of these warnings, then "BLAM," a lightning strike on the nose. It was a very bright flash and caused us to have a loss of vision for 5-6 seconds. It was very similar to being blinded by a photographic flash bulb.

Shortly after the strike, a crew member advised me that there was a loud banging noise on the back side of the fuselage. The strike had burned the insulator of the top antenna. The two-foot long insulator at the end of the antenna wire was banging on the side of the airplane. I was concerned that the pounding of the insulator would create a hole in the pressurized cabin. I requested a descent into Midland, Texas. I started my descent and then the radio operator said he could cut the connection of the antenna and push it out. I said, "Do it." He cut it and pushed it out and the banging stopped. Some farmer near Midland would find a long trailing wire antenna with a large insulator in his cow field. I requested my assigned altitude and proceeded on to San Diego, California.

I examined the aircraft after we landed. We found a large dark burned area on the top of the vertical stabilizer. At the tail, there was melted aluminum about six to eight inches long on both elevators.

Lightning strikes are not uncommon on commercial aircraft. They vary in the amount of damage they cause, but they usually do not disable the aircraft. There have been cases where strikes have downed aircraft. Usually this is when the fuel tanks are very low and the explosion of the tanks caused the plane to crash.

North Island Naval Air Station

1960

My wife and our four children arrived in San Diego after our long driving trip from New York. The first priority was to find a place to stay. We located a three-bedroom house with a one car garage south of the naval air station. It was very convenient and only a few miles from the base. We were pleased with the price. The house had a large back yard with a small banana tree. The price was $13,800. I was outraged that I had to pay an extra $75 to assume the existing loan. Remember this was in the 1950s and prices were a lot lower in those days. We were settled and I could start at the Navy base.

I was assigned as a pilot in the operations department. We had many types of aircraft to fly. A DC-3 transport, a two-engined Cessna Beechcraft, and a larger Convair C-340 cargo transport. The Convair could carry fifty, the twin Beechcraft twelve, and the DC-3 thirty. The Convair was a great airplane. It was powered by two R2800 radial engines that developed 1850 HP each. A very reliable and comfortable plane to fly.

I will relate some of the more interesting events that occurred.

Navy vs Rice in Cotton Bowl! The San Diego Navy Training Station was sending a precision drill team to perform in the Cotton Bowl Classic in Dallas, Texas. I was to fly them there in the Convair C-340. We departed from the North Island Navy Air Station. After getting airborne, there were reports of a dust storm with strong gusting winds in the Dallas area: dust bowl conditions. I landed at El Paso to decide if it was safe to proceed. The dust could do great damage to the engines. I had to make a decision. After being informed that other aircraft were flying, I decided to go. After takeoff, it was like flying in a milk bottle; no clouds, just a dark gray sky. Arriving at night for the approach to the Dallas Airport, due to low visibility, I had to make a radar approach (GCA). The wind was very strong and gusting. On final approach, I encountered a strong downdraft. "We call them sinkers." I had to apply lots of engine power to clear the surrounding airport fence. It was a wild night.

We were given seats on the forty yard line for the game. Navy won, 20 to 7. Roger Staubach was the winning quarterback for Navy. He later became

Convair C-340 factory school San Diego, California. Ski front row, second from left.

famous as the winning quarterback for the Dallas Cowboys in the Superbowl. The Training Station drill team performed well during half time.

We were scheduled to return to San Diego at 0800. Two of the team members were late. I delayed the flight for about twenty minutes. They must have had a wild night. I think I saved the skins of those two late arrivals. The flight back to San Diego was routine.

Patient to Seattle! A sailor with a fractured neck requiring that he be in traction was flown to his home town of Seattle. I flew the Convair C-340 with him on a stretcher. It was necessary that his neck be in constant tension requiring a weight and pulley arrangement. The weight was attached to his skull. It required a rather smooth flight to get him there.

Load to Lompoc Prison! A load of mattress covers was to be delivered to the prison at Lompoc, California. The prisoners were to add an additional two feet to each. After takeoff in the DC-3S, I was alerted to a landing gear unsafe condition. One of my landing gear wheels did not retract. What to do? First, we unloaded the heavy load of mattress covers.

We dropped them in a clear area of the airport. This made the airplane much lighter and easier to handle. I made two approaches bouncing the landing gear tire on the runway. On the third attempt, I successfully received a safe indication of the landing gear. We reloaded the covers and delivered them to the Lompoc prison.

Salton Sea Explosives! Six navy frogmen came aboard the DC-3. I inquired as to what they were there for. They were to blow up stumps for a Salton Sea home. The home happened to be owned by the California congressman. They had two large containers. I asked what was in the boxes? They contained fulminate of mercury detonators. I asked how safe they were. They said they were very safe, but at times they blow up for no reason at all. You could not get those detonators to within three miles of a commercial airliner. I made a very careful, smooth landing.

Special Object! You would never know who would come aboard your airplane. There was a Navy warrant officer with an object with a parachute attached. He also had his personal parachute. I asked what was the object. He said it was a part for an atomic weapon. He was escorting it to the storage area north of Las Vegas. He also told me that if we had to bail out, he would have to bail out with the object. I told him to let me know if he was going to bail out. I would slow down for him.

Overweight DC-3S! I was called on a Sunday to pick up and deliver a maintenance crew to Alameda, California. I arrived at Marine Corps Air Station Miramar and started to load these sailors with all of their gear. They were plane mechanics and had their tool boxes and extra gear. I knew that we were way overweight for safe single engine flight. It was a Sunday and not many options to change the situation. I talked to the chief in charge and

Convair C-340 factory school San Diego, California. Ski at foot of stairs holding rail.

told him we may have to jettison all of the tool boxes and even have the personnel don their chest pack parachutes to lighten the plane if we have an engine failure. The airplane would not be able to maintain altitude with one engine out. Both engines operated satisfactorily and we landed safely in Alameda.

Water rights! It was a Saturday that I received a call from the executive officer of the NAS North Island. He asked me if the Convair C-340 could make it nonstop to Washington, D.C. I told him I would check. I called back and said we would have to land for fuel. I later discovered that he called the Marines. They said they could make it. The trip was for a very important person who had a heart condition, and this was an emergency flight to Bethesda hospital. The Marines had to land short of Washington for fuel and the patient died on board the aircraft.

Secretary of the Navy! I received a call from the executive officer of the NAS North Island. The co-pilot of the secretary's plane had a medical problem and they needed a replacement. I had a C-340 rating and was asked to join the crew. I was in North Island and the crew to join were in an area further north. It was a Sunday morning and the weather was down to zero zero (zero ceiling, zero visibility).

I flew the Twin Beechcraft. This required a takeoff at night with very low visibility. I could only see about two runway lights to keep the plane in the center of the runway. You do this by setting the runway heading on your directional gyro instrument and keeping it on that heading, and maintain a positive rate of climb.

I joined the secretary's crew and stayed with them for ten days. I received a fine letter of appreciation from the Washington VIP transport squadron.

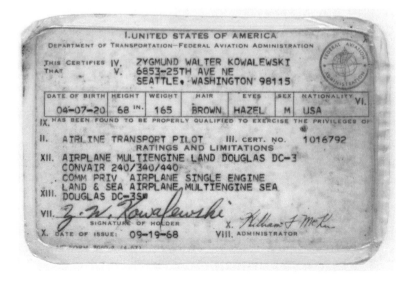

Epilogue

2016

San Diego was my last duty station before retirement. I retired from the Navy after twenty years of service at the early age of forty.

I enjoyed my years in the Navy. I later joined the Federal Aviation Administration and flew as an Airways Systems Inspection Pilot. I moved to Alaska in 1967 and flew for the FAA to all parts of the state for ten years.

I was able to visit many interesting places: from Point Barrow in the far north, to Juneau in the southeast and Shemya at the western end of the Aleutian Chain.

Ski Kowalewski on his retirement day,
Imperial Beach, California, in 1960.

Front, Pat with baby Jim, Kitty and Jane.
Back, Ski, Steve and Bill.

My children are scattered from Arizona to California to Washington with one daughter living in Eagle River, Alaska. My wife passed away in 2014.

I am now retired and in the process of moving from our Anchorage home to the Chugiak-Eagle River Senior Center. Alaska is my permanent home.

Front, Bill, Kitty, Jane.
Back, Steve, Ski, Patricia.

Kitty Rede, daughter.

Ski Kowalewski.

65

GOOD SAM FUND

Chugiak-Eagle River Senior Center

The Good Samaritan (Good Sam) Fund provides help
to senior residents who are in need of assistance.
There are many situations where this fund can help,
including rent, basic needs, emergency medical supplies,
and transportation to health care.

Profits from A Sailor's Life will be donated
to the Good Sam Fund through 2017.

Chugiak-Eagle River Senior Center
22424 N. Birchwood Loop
Chugiak, Alaska 99567